Teaching With Favorite Eric Carle Books

by Joan Novelli

SCHOLASTIC

PROFESSIONAL BOOKS

NEW YORK • TORONTO • LONDON • AUCKLAND • SYDNEY
MEXICO CITY • NEW DELHI • HONG KONG

For Myong-Hee Shim,
our "Very" extraordinary exchange student and friend

We gratefully acknowledge Eric Carle for his lyrical and luminous
contributions to children's literature.

"Caterpillars" from CRICKET IN A THICKET by Aileen Fisher. Copyright © 1963, 1991 by Aileen Fisher.
Used by permission of Marian Reiner for the author.

"Cat Kisses" by Bobbi Katz. Copyright © 1974 and renewed 1996 by Bobbi Katz. Reprinted by permission of the author.

"Ladybug Rhyme" from BIG POETRY ANIMALS by Maria Fleming. Copyright © 1996 by Maria Fleming.
Used by permission of Scholastic Professional Books.

"Winter Moon" by Langston Hughes. From COLLECTED POEMS by Langston Hughes.
Copyright © 1994 by the Estate of Langston Hughes. Reprinted by permission of Alfred A. Knopf, a division of Random House.

"Yellow Weed" by Lilian Moore. From LITTLE RACCOON AND POEMS FROM THE WOODS by Lilian Moore.
Copyright © 1972 by Lilian Moore. Reprinted by permission of Marian Reiner for the author.

Photograph of Eric Carle by S. Petegorsky, page 5, courtesy of Penguin Putnam Books for Young Readers.

THE TINY SEED, book jacket and flower art (book cover and page 34): Reprinted with the permission of Simon & Schuster Books for Young Readers,
an imprint of Simon & Schuster Children's Publishing Division from THE TINY SEED by Eric Carle. Copyright © 1987 by Eric Carle Corp.

HAVE YOU SEEN MY CAT?, book jacket (page 18): Reprinted with the permission of Simon & Schuster Books for Young Readers,
an imprint of Simon & Schuster Children's Publishing Division from HAVE YOU SEEN MY CAT? by Eric Carle. Copyright © 1987 by Eric Carle Corp.

PAPA, PLEASE GET THE MOON FOR ME, book jacket (page 44): Reprinted with the permission of Simon & Schuster Books for Young Readers, an imprint of
Simon & Schuster Children's Publishing Division from PAPA, PLEASE GET THE MOON FOR ME by Eric Carle. Copyright © 1986 by Eric Carle Corp.

A HOUSE FOR HERMIT CRAB, book jacket, fish art, border art (pages 8, 10, 12, 15, 16, 19, 23, 26, 41, 46, 49, 53, 57, 58; border art pages 1, 3-64):
Reprinted with the permission of Simon & Schuster Books for Young Readers, an imprint of Simon & Schuster Children's Publishing Division from PAPA,
PLEASE GET THE MOON FOR ME by Eric Carle. Copyright © 1986 by Eric Carle Corp.

THE VERY HUNGRY CATERPILLAR, book jacket and caterpillar art (book cover and pages 3, 4, 6, 7, 9, 10, 16, 19, 23, 28, 36, 40, 45, 50, 54, 57, 61):
Reprinted with the permission of Penguin Putnam Books for Young Readers from THE VERY HUNGRY CATERPILLAR by Eric Carle.
Copyright © 1969 by Eric Carle Corp.

THE VERY BUSY SPIDER, book jacket and spider art (pages 11, 24, 29, 35, 39, 46): Reprinted with the permission of Penguin Putnam Books for Young Readers
from THE VERY BUSY SPIDER by Eric Carle. Copyright © 1984 by Eric Carle Corp.

THE VERY LONELY FIREFLY, book jacket and firefly art (page 56): Reprinted with the permission of Penguin Putnam Books for Young Readers from
THE VERY LONELY FIREFLY by Eric Carle. Copyright © 1995 by Eric Carle Corp.

THE VERY CLUMSY CLICK BEETLE, book jacket and click beetle art (pages 9, 14, 18, 22, 27, 34, 39, 44, 49, 52, 56, 60): Reprinted with the permission of
Penguin Putnam Books for Young Readers from THE VERY CLUMSY CLICK BEETLE by Eric Carle. Copyright © 1999 by Eric Carle Corp.

TODAY IS MONDAY, book jacket (page 52): Reprinted with the permission of Penguin Putnam Books for Young Readers from
TODAY IS MONDAY by Eric Carle. Copyright © 1993 by Eric Carle Corp.

THE GROUCHY LADYBUG, book jacket and ladybug art (book cover and pages 5, 12, 16, 20, 24, 27, 30, 36, 41, 47, 50, 54, 58, 62):
Reprinted with the permission of HarperCollins from THE GROUCHY LADYBUG by Eric Carle. Copyright © 1977 by Eric Carle Corp.

THE MIXED-UP CHAMELEON, book jacket (page 22): Reprinted with the permission of HarperCollins from
THE MIXED-UP CHAMELEON by Eric Carle. Copyright © 1975 by Eric Carle Corp.

PANCAKES, PANCAKES, book jacket (page 14): Reprinted from PANCAKES, PANCAKES by Eric Carle (Knopf). Copyright © 1970 by Eric Carle Corp.

Cover design by Sue Kass
Interior design by Solutions by Design, Inc.
Interior art by James Graham Hale

ISBN: 0-439-19102-5

# Contents

About This Book

"I believe that children are naturally creative and eager to learn," says Eric Carle. "I want to show them that learning is really both fascinating and fun." (from Biographical Notes for Eric Carle, www.eric-carle.com) Through dozens of books, Eric Carle inspires children's creativity and desire to learn. Positive messages about confidence, courage, hope, compassion, perseverance, and other life lessons gently find their way from his books into children's hearts and minds. His collage illustrations appeal to the tactile side of the way children learn—the sense of touch that tells them so much about their world.

The Very Hungry Caterpillar, though not Eric Carle's first book, is the one that launched his trademark style. Published in 1969 and translated into more than 25 languages, this celebrated classic has wiggled its way into the hearts and homes of millions of children. Like *The Very Hungry Caterpillar*, Eric Carle's books have a way of instantly connecting with children—and remaining as favorites with all ages. Through simple text and enchanting collage illustrations, the books capture the innate curiosity children have for the world around them—from their wonder about the way the moon seems to change shape to their interest in the tiny creatures that make their homes under stones and beneath bark.

In the pages that follow, you'll find activities for extending the learning that comes naturally with Eric Carle's books. Pages 6 to 8 suggest ideas that you can use with any of the books. Pages 9 to 64 feature activities for individual titles, including:

- ★ vocabulary-building games
- ★ fun phonics lessons
- ★ poems to share
- ★ hands-on math activities
- ★ science investigations
- ★ interactive displays
- ★ movement games
- ★ art projects
- ★ and more!

> Eric Carle's "Very" books are interactive! Each has a special treat in store for readers. The spider's web in *The Very Busy Spider* is raised, letting children feel the web as the spider spins. The quiet cricket chirps, thanks to a tiny computer chip inside the back cover. *The Very Lonely Firefly* has a tiny battery that supplies power to light up the fireflies on the last page, and *The Very Clumsy Click Beetle* clicks as the star of the story flips through the air!

About Eric Carle

Photograph by S. Petegorsky.

That Eric Carle's books are so universally appealing to children is no surprise. His work is based in large part on his own childhood. "When I was a small boy," he says, "my father would take me on walks across meadows and through woods. He would lift a stone or peel back the bark of a tree and show me the living things that scurried about. He'd tell me about the life cycles of this or that small creature and then he would carefully put the little creature back into its home." (from www.eric-carle.com) Carle recaptures those treasured childhood experiences in his books, with words and pictures that invite his young readers to make connections to their own thoughts and feelings.

Eric Carle was born in Syracuse, New York in 1929. He moved to Germany with his parents when he was six years old. After spending the next 17 years in Germany, he returned to America to begin a career in art. He worked as a graphic designer with *The New York Times* and as an art director for an advertising agency. His career in children's books began when author Bill Martin, Jr. saw a lobster Carle had created for an advertisement. The two collaborated on what became a favorite with children—*Brown Bear, Brown Bear, What Do You See?* Carle soon wrote and illustrated his own book—*1, 2, 3 to the Zoo. The Very Hungry Caterpillar* and dozens of other books followed, each adding to the distinctive voice and artistic style that make Carle's books unforgettable.

LEARN MORE

Books

The Art of Eric Carle by Eric Carle (Philomel, 1996). This rich resource contains autobiographical information that you can share with students, pictures of the author throughout his life, full-page illustrations from books, and more.

Flora and Tiger: 19 Very Short Stories From My Life by Eric Carle (Putnam, 1997). These personal vignettes give readers a glimpse into the ways animals, friends, and family shaped Eric Carle's life and work.

My Apron: A Story From My Childhood by Eric Carle (Putnam, 1995). Eric Carle recalls summer days spent working with his uncle, a plasterer. They both wore aprons with a pocket, and a child-size one is included with the book.

Video

The Eric Carle Picture Writer Video (Putnam; ISBN: 0-399-22624-9; $39.99). Visit Eric Carle in his studio, listen to him read his books, and watch him create his trademark tissue-paper collage. For more information call (800) 631-8571.

Web Sites

The Official Eric Carle Web Site (**www.eric-carle.com**): This easy-to-navigate site contains biographical information, as well as answers to questions children often ask about the author's books.

Children's Book Council (**www.cbcbooks.org**): Click on "Meet the Authors" for a link to information about Eric Carle.

Activities for Any Time

In addition to the activities suggested for each Eric Carle title featured in this book, try any of the following ideas to enhance your students' literature-based experiences.

Books in a Box

Eric Carle collects story and illustration ideas in a box. When he's ready to start a new book, he sifts through the ideas to find the right one. Let students make "idea boxes" to gather their own story ideas. Have them decorate and label shoeboxes. Discuss possible sources of story ideas. Many writers, including Eric Carle, look for ideas in the world around them. For example, the inspiration for Carle's many books about bugs came from walks he took as a child with his father. Students will discover story ideas in their everyday lives—in conversations and events, in family routines and special occasions. They can also collect unusual objects and cut out pictures from magazines and newspapers that may inspire future stories. Have students store their ideas in their boxes. When they're ready to start a new story, they'll have a box full of inspiration!

Planning an Author Study

You may choose to share an Eric Carle book simply to enjoy a favorite story with your students. Or, you may select a title that supports a teaching topic—for example, *The Very Hungry Caterpillar* goes well with a unit on life cycles or butterflies. Students also enjoy getting to know an author in depth—reading several books and making comparisons between illustrations, characters, themes, and so on. To set up an Eric Carle author study, gather multiple copies of several titles. You might start with the "Very" books (*The Very Hungry Caterpillar, The Very Busy Spider, The Very Clumsy Click Beetle,* etc.). Share the stories over a period of time. Use Venn diagrams to compare books. Ask questions to guide children in a discussion—for example:

- 🌟 How is [title] like [title]?
- 🌟 In what ways are the characters alike?
- 🌟 In what ways are the characters different?
- 🌟 Are there ways you are like one of the characters in these books?
- 🌟 What is something the characters in each book learn? Do you think the author wants you to learn something, too?

Putting on Mini-Plays

Dramatizations are also a wonderful way for children to demonstrate their understanding of a story. Many students enjoy acting out favorite stories—with or without props. Some Eric Carle books, such as *The Very Hungry Caterpillar*, are just right for children to dramatize on their own. Others, such as *The Very Grouchy Ladybug*, call for a cast of characters. Let students create simple props for acting out Eric Carle stories—black construction-paper dots taped to a red shirt make a grouchy or friendly ladybug, flashlights light up a room for a production of *The Very Lonely Firefly*, and a pan and spatula let children act out *Pancakes, Pancakes*. Students can create more elaborate productions, too, using large sheets of paper to create backdrops. Share these tips with students as they rehearse their parts.

- 🌟 Practice projecting your voice. Can your classmates hear you across the room?
- 🌟 Stand facing your audience. This will make it easier to hear what you say.
- 🌟 Use facial expressions to show how your character feels.

Make a Map

Where do the characters in Eric Carle's books live? Let children map their neighborhoods—from the leafy, green world of *The Very Hungry Caterpillar* to the farm of the boy in *Pancakes, Pancakes*. Encourage children to map as many details as they can from the stories.

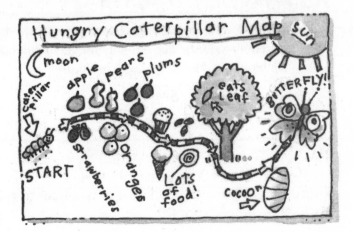

An Art Lesson

Eric Carle combines bold colors and simple shapes to create rich collage illustrations that appeal to children of all ages. Collage is a rewarding technique for young children to try themselves. The tactile nature of the art form is appealing to many children, who learn much through the sense of touch. The open-endedness of collage also frees up many children who may feel less successful with other art forms. For example, young children who have not yet developed the fine motor coordination to handle pencils and paintbrushes with ease will happily tear paper to create glorious collages.

After sharing books by Eric Carle, invite students to study the illustrations closely. What can they tell about his art? Guide them to notice how pieces of paper are layered to create the people, places, objects, and creatures in the illustrations. Pass around some tissue paper, then explain that Eric Carle prepares his own tissue paper for his pictures. He paints the tissue paper, adding the patterns and splashes of color students see. He then tears and cuts out shapes and glues them into place on illustration board.

Let students create their own collages, using characters or scenes from a story for inspiration, or coming up with their own. Provide assorted supplies, including:

★ sturdy drawing paper or illustration board

★ tissue paper in assorted colors, as well as in white

★ scissors

★ glue

★ paints, paintbrushes

★ sponges, toothbrushes, jar lids, plastic forks, and other tools (for applying paint to the tissue paper and creating assorted textures)

★ crayons

Have students cut and tear the paper into shapes, layering shapes and colors to create a collage. Have them glue the papers in place and add additional details with crayon if they wish.

 **Tips**

◎ To more easily manage supplies, have children use trays or shoebox lids to gather and store their collage materials and artworks in progress.

◎ Children can use reclosable sandwich bags to store paper that they've cut up but not yet used.

◎ To keep your art center well stocked, invite families to send in collage materials, such as used tissue paper from gifts.

THE VERY
HUNGRY
CATERPILLAR
by Eric Carle

The Very Hungry Caterpillar

(Philomel, 1969)

"In the light of the moon a little egg lay on a leaf." This celebrated classic, the first in a quintet of "Very" books, is a favorite with all ages. A hungry caterpillar emerges from its little egg and proceeds to eat through an assortment of foods, which results in a stomachache by week's end. This book is more than a counting book. In charming simplicity, it reveals lessons about the wonders of nature and life.

BEFORE READING

Who's Hungry?

Students will guess by the title that the caterpillar in this story is going to have something to eat. What will it be? Invite children to guess. Let them tell about foods they like to eat when they too are hungry.

Caterpillar Science

A caterpillar is one of those creatures that children seem to be instinctively drawn to. Is it the way the tiny creature wiggles its way from one place to another? Or is it the mystery of metamorphosis—the idea that the caterpillar will somehow turn into a butterfly one day? Let children share comments about caterpillars—what they think about them, know about them, and so on. If you plan on having a caterpillar in the classroom for students to observe, now is a good time to introduce it. (See Learn More, page 12.)

CONCEPTS and THEMES

◎ counting

◎ life cycles, changes

◎ nature

◎ nutrition

Word Play

Revisit the story, asking students to look for words that name foods, including:

apple
pears
plums
strawberries
oranges
chocolate cake
ice cream cone
pickle
Swiss cheese
salami
lollipop
cherry pie
sausage
cupcake
watermelon
"one nice green leaf"

Record these on pieces of paper cut in the shape of each food. Let children match the words for days of the week with the foods, based on what the caterpillar ate and when.

 **Tip**

Check for food allergies before serving Caterpillar Snacks.

Book Talk

It's a toss-up—will students want to talk about the caterpillar's diet, which included cake, ice cream, and other yummy treats, or will they want to discuss the magical change that occurs at the end of the story? In either case, they may also notice something about the author's word choice at the end: The butterfly emerges from a "cocoon," not a chrysalis. Eric Carle explains his word choice. He says, "In most cases a butterfly does come from a chrysalis, but not all. There's a rare genus called Parnassian, that pupates in a cocoon. These butterflies live in the Pacific Northwest, in Siberia, and as far away as North Korea and the northern islands of Japan." Students will enjoy hearing his "unscientific" explanation for the word choice, too. "…when I was a small boy, my father would say, 'Eric, come out of your cocoon.' He meant I should open up and be receptive to the world around me. For me, it would not sound right to say, 'Come out of your chrysalis.' And so poetry won over science!" (from **www.eric-carle.com**)

MATH, SCIENCE

Monarch Miles

What do your students know about migrating animals? Invite them to share information—for example, they may know that some birds fly south in winter and that whales move to warmer waters when cold weather comes. Ask: *How do you think butterflies stay warm in winter?* Explain that, like birds and whales, some butterflies travel south, or *migrate*. Monarchs head south by the millions, making their way to Florida and Mexico. For some, this is a 2,000-mile journey. Help students get a sense of this distance with this hands-on activity.

★ Measure a quarter mile on the playground or sidewalk area outside the school. Ask: *How many times would we have to walk this distance to go one mile?* (four)

★ Let students "migrate" one mile in a butterfly's journey by walking the marked-off quarter-mile four times. Ask: *How many more times would we have to repeat this to travel as far as a monarch?* (1,999) Help students find Florida and Mexico on a map. Use the scale of miles to mark spots that are approximately 2,000 miles away.

MATH

Caterpillar Snacks

Plan a snack of the foods the hungry caterpillar ate—and provide practice with sequencing at the same time. Invite families to sign up to send in each food—enough for a bite or two for each child. Cut the foods into bite-size pieces. Give children paper plates and let them take samples of the foods. Have children arrange the foods on their plates in the order in which the caterpillar ate them. (You can use leafy lettuce for the green leaf in the story.)

Amazing Changes Wheel

Butterflies undergo *complete metamorphosis*—they go through four changes, from egg to larva to pupa to adult. Insects that undergo complete metamorphosis don't look anything like the adult version when they are in the larva stage. Let children represent the changes in a butterfly's life with this activity.

- Have children trace and cut out circles from sturdy paper (about 8 to 10 inches in diameter).

- Ask children to divide their circles into four equal sections, as shown, and write the name of each life cycle stage in a section.

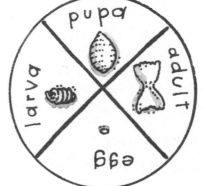

- Give each child four pasta shapes: orzo, spiral, shell, and bowtie. Have them decide which shape looks most like each life cycle stage and glue it in that section.

Butterfly or Moth?

Butterflies and moths have much in common—for example, they have a similar shape as adults. Display an assortment of pictures of both butterflies and moths. (Check nature magazines.) Ask students to sort the pictures into two groups: those they think are butterflies and those they think are moths. Encourage them to share their reasons for placing pictures in one group or another. Then share these tips for telling the two apart.

- Butterflies rest with their wings folded up vertically.

- Moths rest with their wings spread out.

- Butterflies have long antennae with knobs at the end.

- Moths have fuzzy-looking feelers.

   Let children take another look at the two groups. One by one, have them reevaluate the placement based on the new information they have. Be sure to have students give reasons for moving any of the pictures from one group to the other.

Cecropia Moth

at rest

Silvery Blue Butterfly

at rest

POETRY BREAK

Copy the poem "Caterpillars" (see page 13) on sentence strips and place in a pocket chart. Read it aloud with students a couple of times, then cut off the last word in each line. Place these words to the side in the pocket chart and read the poem again. This time, let students take turns choosing the word to complete each line. Encourage children to use the rhyming words as clues. Give each child a copy of the poem. Have children complete the activities on the page to learn more.

 **Tip**

Have children research the life cycles of other insects—for example, ants, beetles, dragonflies, bees, moths, and wasps.

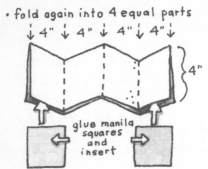

- 8"×16" paper folded lengthwise
- fold again into 4 equal parts
  ↓ 4" ↓ 4" ↓ 4" ↓ 4" ↓

} 4"

glue manila squares and insert

Life-Cycle Fold-and-Flip Book

This book is fun to make and to read. One side lets students tell what they know about a butterfly's life cycle. They flip the book to tell what they know about stages in their own lives. Follow these directions to prepare each blank book.

✦ Cut sturdy white paper to 8 by 16 inches.

✦ Fold the paper in half lengthwise, then into four equal sections.

✦ Cut two squares from a manila folder, just a little under 8 square inches each. Place glue on both sides of the manila folder squares and place them inside the two end sections of the book. (This reinforces the front and back covers.)

To create their books, have students write what they know about a butterfly's life cycle on one side of the book. Have them flip the book upside down and over, then tell what they know about stages in their own lives. They can illustrate the stages in a butterfly's life, and use photos or pictures to illustrate the stages in their own lives.

🐞 LEARN MORE

Books

The Butterfly Alphabet by Kjell B. Sandved (Scholastic, 1996). Children will delight in looking for letters of the alphabet hidden in the wondrous wings of butterflies.

Butterfly Story by Anca Hariton (Dutton, 1995). Beginning with a butterfly laying one tiny egg on a leaf, this book shares the science of metamorphosis.

"The First Butterfly" from *Keepers of the Animals* by Michael J. Caduto and Joseph Bruchac (Fulcrum, 1991). This Native American folk tale explains how the first butterflies came to be.

Ride the Wind: Airborne Journeys of Animals and Plants by Seymour Simon (Harcourt Brace, 1997). Learn about monarchs' amazing journeys, including the "butterfly trees" they settle on by the millions.

Software and Video

Geo Kids: Tadpoles, Dragonflies, and the Caterpillar's Big Change (National Geographic). If your students can't observe the real transformation from caterpillar to butterfly, this video is the next best thing.

One Small Square: Backyard (Freeman, 1993). Based on the acclaimed series by Donald Silver, this program invites children to discover the world around them. It includes a close-up look at butterflies.

Web Sites

Journey North (**www.learner.org**): Join more than 4,500 schools from the 50 states and beyond to track seasonal change and migration. Students share field observations, with scientists providing expertise directly to the classroom along the way.

Other

To order butterfly larva: Insect Lore, P.O. Box 1535, Shafter, CA 93263, (800) LIVE-BUG; and The Butterfly Place, P.O. Box 1541, 120 Tyngsboro Rd., Westford, MA 01886, (978) 392-0955.

Name _____ Date _____

Caterpillars

What do caterpillars do?
Nothing much but chew and chew.

What do caterpillars know?
Nothing much but how to grow.

They just eat what by and by
will make them be a butterfly.

But that is more than I can do
however much I chew and chew.

—Aileen Fisher

Try this!

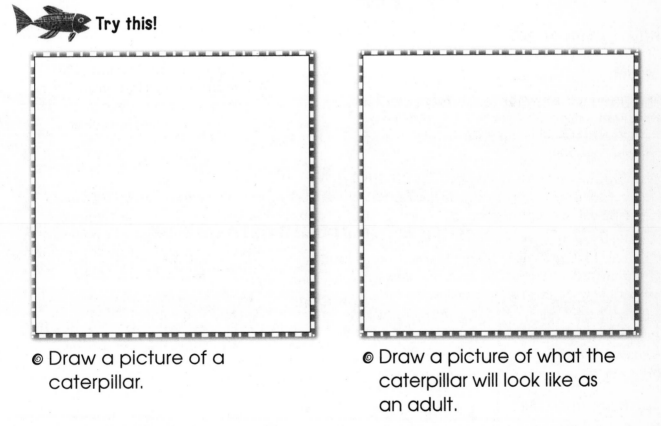

◎ Draw a picture of a
caterpillar.

◎ Draw a picture of what the
caterpillar will look like as
an adult.

On the back of this paper, draw a picture of you. Then draw a picture
of what you can be when you are an adult!

Pancakes, Pancakes

(Knopf, 1970)

Jack's hungry for pancakes, but first he must cut and grind the wheat to make flour, fetch the egg, milk the cow, churn cream into butter, build a fire for cooking, and get jam from the cellar. With everything assembled, it's time to measure, mix, and cook. Step-by-step text takes readers from putting flour in the bowl to popping pancakes in the mouth.

CONCEPTS and THEMES

- ⊚ cooperation
- ⊚ families
- ⊚ farm life
- ⊚ following directions

BEFORE READING

What's for Breakfast?

Introduce this story by taking a quick class poll: *Who ate pancakes for breakfast this morning?* Let children share how their pancake breakfast was made—for example, by placing frozen pancakes in the toaster, or by mixing up batter from scratch. Let children share other foods they ate for breakfast and how those foods were prepared.

What's in a Pancake?

Before reading the story, ask: *What ingredients do you think will go into the pancakes that the boy in this story eats?* Record guesses, then encourage children to listen carefully to find out.

Book Talk

Were there any surprises in this story? Ask the following questions to elicit children's reactions.

★ How many pancake ingredients did Jack's mother use? How many did we think she would need?

★ What do Jack and his mother do differently from your family or people you know when they cook pancakes? *(they churn their own butter, cook over a fire,* and so on.)

★ What did Jack put on his pancakes? *(jam)* What do you like on yours?

LANGUAGE ARTS

Flipping Flapjacks

A few simple props make learning word families lots of fun. Gather a griddle or frying pan and a spatula, then cook up some word-family pancakes.

★ Glue white construction paper to brown construction paper. Cut out circles about three inches in diameter.

★ On the brown side of each pancake, write a word that belongs to a word family you want to teach. Look for words in the book to make a connection with the text—for example, *pancake*. (Write words such as *bake, Jake, lake, make, rake, take,* and *wake* on the pancake patterns.)

★ Write the word family (such as *–ake*) on the white side of each pancake.

★ Place the pancakes word-side down on a griddle or in a frying pan. Let children take turns flipping the pancakes and reading the word on each.

LANGUAGE ARTS

Writing Recipes

Revisit the pages in the book that show Jack and his mother making the pancakes. Follow up by making a class cookbook of favorite breakfast foods. Let children choose a food, then write directions for preparing it. Encourage children to think through the steps in the process before writing (or dictating) the recipe. Before they begin, share some sample recipes. Ask: *What makes these recipes easy to follow?* Point out lists of ingredients and numbered steps. Have children illustrate their recipes, then put them together to make a class book.

 **Tip**

To make copies of the class cookbook to share at home, arrange several recipes on one page (front and back) and make two-sided copies.

Word Play

Revisit the story, asking children to notice all the words that show what the boy does—for example, *cut, grind, fetch, churn,* and *build.* Ask: *How are these words alike?* (They show what the boy is doing.) Explain that these kinds of words are called *verbs*—they describe actions. Invite children to share other verbs, such as *walk, talk,* and *read.*

 **Tip**

For a special touch, make pancakes in fun shapes. Set cookie cutters on the griddle and pour batter inside them. Remove the cookie cutters when the pancakes are ready to flip.

MATH

Who Likes Pancakes?

How many students prefer pancakes for breakfast? Make a class graph to find out. Start by brainstorming favorite breakfast foods. Try to include a selection that represents a variety of cultures. Let children register their favorites on the graph by writing their name on a graph marker and placing it in the corresponding column. Extend the graph to include other classes in the same grade or hall, or the entire school. Let children make predictions first, based on results of the class graph.

MATH, SCIENCE, LANGUAGE ARTS

Measure, Mix, and Pour

Cook up some pancakes in the classroom to explore the science of change. Students will strengthen sequencing, measuring, predicting, and communicating skills in the process.

- Start by giving each child a copy of page 17. Ask: *What is wrong with this recipe?* (The steps are scrambled.) Let children cut out each sentence strip and arrange the steps in order. Have them glue the strips in order on a sheet of paper.

- Gather ingredients for pancakes. (A boxed pancake mix will also provide for plenty of learning.)

- Copy the directions on chart paper. Read them aloud as you guide students in following them. Look for science and math skill-building opportunities along the way. For example, if you mix pancake mix with water, ask: *Do you think one cup of dry pancake mix and one cup of water will equal two cups of pancake batter?*

- As you cook the pancakes, encourage children to observe changes—for example, they may notice that tiny bubbles form, that the batter puffs up and browns, and that the batter turns to a solid.

 **LEARN MORE**

Books

Pancakes for Breakfast by Tomie de Paola (Harcourt Brace, 1990). In this wordless picture book, a little old lady tries to make pancakes but a couple of things—including her pets—get in the way.

Hey Kids, You're Cookin' Now: A Global Awareness Cooking Adventure by Dianne Pratt (Harvest Hill, 1998). Add cooking to your classroom activities with this colorfully illustrated book. Includes lots of kid-friendly treats, and ecological connections.

Web Sites

Kids Kitchen (**www.scoreone.com/cgi-bin/ kids_queries/messes2.cfm**): Find favorite kid recipes here, including one for ice cream pancakes!

Measure, Mix, and Pour

Then stir the milk mixture into the flour mixture. (It's okay if there are some lumps.)

Next put 2 cups flour in a separate bowl.

Finally, cook the pancakes on both sides. Eat them!

Add 2 teaspoons baking powder, 1 teaspoon baking soda, 1 tablespoon sugar, and a pinch of salt to the flour.

First mix 2 cups buttermilk with 2 eggs and 2 tablespoons melted butter.

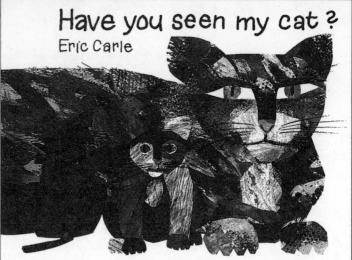

Have You Seen My Cat?

(Simon & Schuster, 1987)

"Have you seen my cat?" a boy asks a man, who points him in the direction of a lion. "This is not *my* cat!" the boy responds. This happens again and again, as the boy's search turns up all kinds of cats—a bobcat, a puma, a jaguar, a panther, a tiger, a cheetah, and finally, his own.

CONCEPTS and THEMES

◎ perseverance

◎ responsibility

◎ animal families

BEFORE READING

All Kinds of Cats

How many different kinds of cats do students know? Let them name them, including various kinds of house cats (tiger, long-haired, short-haired, and so on). Record names on chart paper. Ask students to look for these and other cats in the story.

Pet Stories

Children love to share stories from their own lives. In preparation for this story, they'll enjoy telling about their pets. Students without pets can tell about friends', neighbors', and relatives' pets. To keep the stories moving along, tell students that they can each have one minute to share a story. (You'd be surprised at how much can be told in a minute.) Sound a ten-second "meow" to let students know they need to finish up.

Book Talk

How do students think the boy feels at the beginning of the story? at the end? How about each time he checks out a different cat, only to find that it is not his cat? Discuss the various feelings the boy might experience—for example, *worried*, *disappointed*, and *relieved*—then let students share times they have had the same feelings. They might recall times their own pets have been missing, or think of other events that resulted in similar feelings.

LANGUAGE ARTS

Ask and Answer

Divide the class into two groups, one for each repeating line in the story ("Have you seen my cat?" and "This is not *my* cat!"). Let students practice their lines with their groups. Reread the story, letting children chime in on their lines as the search for the missing cat continues. Read the story again, letting each group read the other line.

LANGUAGE ARTS

Punctuation Mark Hunt

Introduce the use of question marks by taking another look at the title of this book: *Have You Seen My Cat?* Ask: *What is this kind of sentence called?* (question) *Do you know the name of the punctuation mark at the end of the sentence?* (question mark) Let students practice using question marks by including questions in a Daily Letter. Leave out the punctuation. Let children decide which sentences need periods and which need question marks. Go further by letting students copy sentences from books they're reading, again leaving out the punctuation. Let them exchange papers and add question marks as needed.

LANGUAGE ARTS

Showing Special Words

"This is not *my* cat!" the boy in the story responds over and over as he looks for his cat. Write this sentence on the chalkboard, including the italics for the word *my*. Ask children what they notice about the word *my*. (*They might notice that it slants.*) Explain that this type is called *italic* and is sometimes used by writers to put emphasis on a word. Let students take turns reading aloud this sentence, placing emphasis on the word *my*. Let them try reading the sentence aloud without the italics. Which do they like better? Challenge children to find examples of italic type in other books. Use their findings to introduce other reasons to use italics—for example, in titles, to indicate a word in a foreign language, or to show a word that is being defined.

Word Play

How many names for different kinds of cats can students find? Let them revisit the story, identifying those words and recording them on chart paper. Words include, in order:

lion
bobcat
puma
jaguar
panther
tiger
cheetah

Share pictures of different kinds of cats and let students compare one to another.

 **Tip**

If you have a computer, show students how to select italic-style type. Let children take turns typing in sentences and making one of the words italic.

LANGUAGE ARTS

Missing Cat Matching Game

Encourage descriptive writing skills with a matching game.

★ Start by giving each child a cat pattern to color. (See page 21.) Encourage children to add plenty of detail by using a variety of colors and patterns. You might share pictures of cats to give students ideas.

★ Give each child a sheet of plain paper. Have children write the word "Missing" at the top of the paper and write sentences that describe their cats underneath.

★ Attach a piece of Velcro® to the back of each cat and to the bottom of each Missing poster.

★ Display Missing posters. Mix up the cats and give one to each child. Have children "find" each missing cat by looking for the description that best matches their cat. Have them stick each cat to its matching poster.

Missing!
My cat has orange ears and a striped tail.
She has two stripes on her front legs, and different colored spots on her body: they are orange and brown and yellow.

🕷 LEARN MORE

Books

Annie and the Wild Animals by Jan Brett (Houghton Mifflin, 1985). Annie's cat disappears, so she tries to make friends with assorted woodland creatures. *Publisher's Weekly* says, "The pictures hold countless surprises. Indisputably, this is a work of wonder…"

Big Cats by Seymour Simon (HarperCollins, 1994). Learn how seven big cats hunt, care for their young, and more. Colorful photos capture the cats in action.

The Cookie-Store Cat by Cynthia Rylant (Scholastic, 1999). A skinny cat is adopted by the cookie-store bakers. Children will have great fun following the recipes at the end of the book for Gumdrop Gems,

Frosty Fruit Squares, Cinnamon Sugarplums, and other cookies mentioned in the book.

How Many Spots Does a Leopard Have? and Other Tales by Julius Lester (Scholastic, 1989). Universal messages of courage and loyalty come through in this illustrated collection of 12 folk tales.

I Am the Cat by Lee Bennett Hopkins (Harcourt Brace, 1981). This pleasing collection of poems will inspire your young poets to write about their pets.

Web Sites

Cats! Wild to Mild (**www.nhm.org/cats/teacher/index.htm**): Get cat facts or download a complete cat curriculum.

Missing Cat Matching Game

The Mixed-Up Chameleon

(HarperCollins, 1975)

The Mixed-Up Chameleon
by Eric Carle

A dissatisfied chameleon visits a zoo and wishes to be like all sorts of animals—big and white like a polar bear, handsome like a flamingo, smart like a fox, and so on. The chameleon changes with each wish, but in the end decides he'd rather be himself.

CONCEPTS and THEMES

- self-concept
- changes
- camouflage

BEFORE READING

Using Picture Clues

Let students use the picture on the cover to help read the word *chameleon*. If they substitute *lizard*, praise their good guess, then ask what letter they hear at the beginning of *lizard*. Help students see that the word on the cover starts with the letter *c*. Let them try again, then read the word *chameleon*. Clap the syllables in the word and read it again together. You might ask students to give you a sign (such as waving their hands) each time they hear the word when you read the story aloud.

Chameleons Change Color

Set the scene for the story by asking children what they know about chameleons. Guide students to understand that chameleons can change color to match their surroundings. You might introduce the word *camouflage* and let students share what they know about it.

Book Talk

The message in this story comes through loud and clear—*be yourself*. Ask children why they think the chameleon wanted to be all the other animals. In the end, why did he want to be himself? Invite children to share times they've wanted to be like someone else. Let them share the things they like best about being themselves—inside and out.

SCIENCE

Now You See Me, Now You Don't

Camouflage is one of the ways animals stay safe from predators. Animals that can blend with their surroudings are more difficult for predators to spot. Camouflage helps predators, too. Animals that can blend in with their surroundings can get closer to their prey. Here's a simple activity to help students discover how camouflage works.

* Give each child two pieces of wallpaper and a small chameleon pattern. (You can reduce the templates on page 25.) Try to use an assortment of wallpaper patterns, but make sure each child has two pieces of the same pattern.

* Have children trace the chameleon on one piece of wallpaper as many times as they can and cut them out.

* Have children glue the wallpaper chameleons to the second piece of wallpaper.

* Display the camouflaged chameleons. How many can children find on each piece of wallpaper?

LANGUAGE ARTS

Words That Describe

Introduce adjectives by taking another look at the title, *The Mixed-Up Chameleon*. Ask: *What word in the title describes the chameleon?* (mixed-up) Explain that words like *mixed-up* are called *adjectives*. An adjective is a word that describes a person, place, or thing. Let students take turns using words that describe things in the classroom—for example, *cozy reading corner*, *open windows*, and *busy children*. Follow up by sending students on a scavenger hunt to find adjectives in books and other reading material. Bring students together to share their findings. Start an adjective word wall that students can use when they're looking for just the right describing word.

Word Play

Invite students to look for words in the story that tell what the chameleon wants to be, including:

◎ **big and white like a polar bear**

◎ **handsome like a flamingo**

◎ **smart like a fox**

◎ **strong like an elephant**

Record descriptions on chart paper and use as a springboard to exploring descriptive writing.

 **Tip**

Check paint and home-decorating stores for wallpaper samples and scraps.

POETRY BREAK

Encourage your students to celebrate who they are with the poem "Celebrating Me." (See page 26.) After reading the poem aloud a couple of times, invite students to chime in on the words ME I AM.

SCIENCE, ART

Color Changers

Your students can make color-changing chameleons of their own with this activity.

Materials

chameleon pattern (see page 25)	paper towels
paper	measuring spoons
purple grape juice	baking soda
paper cups	water
cotton swabs	vinegar

1 Give each child a pattern page to color and cut out. Have children arrange their chameleons on paper and add scenery if they wish.

2 Give each group of students a cup of grape juice and some cotton swabs. Have students paint their chameleons with the juice. Let dry.

3 For each group, mix 1 tablespoon baking soda and 3 tablespoons water in one cup. Place vinegar in a second cup. Label the cups.

4 Have students use cotton swabs to paint designs on their chameleons with the baking soda mixture and the vinegar. Have them use clean cotton swabs for each and be careful not to overlap the baking soda and vinegar.

5 Talk about the changes students observe. Guide students to understand that chemical reactions cause changes to occur. In this case, grape juice contains a chemical that changes color based on a substance's acidity (or pH). A *base*, such as baking soda, will cause it to turn bluish-green. An *acid*, such as vinegar, will cause it to turn pink. (Note: A real chameleon changes color because of changes in its skin cells. A chameleon's skin has layers of color cells. Each layer is responsible for a color. When a chameleon changes color, one layer expands while another shrinks. For more information, see Learn More, below.)

Adapted from ScienceArt *by Deborah Schecter (Scholastic Professional Books, 1997).*

 **LEARN MORE**

Books

Chameleons: Dragons in the Trees by James Martin (Crown, 1991). Learn about chameleons, including why and how they change color.

Chameleon Was a Spy by Diane Redfield Massie (Crowell, 1979). When a pickle company's magic formula disappears, superspy Chameleon comes to the rescue. Share some pickles as you read aloud

this entertaining tale. Try other titles in the series, too, including *Chameleon the Spy and the Terrible Toaster Trap* and *Chameleon the Spy and the Case of the Vanishing Jewels.*

Crafty Chameleon by Mwenye Hadithi (Little, Brown, 1984). This trickster tale tells how a chameleon tricks a leopard and crocodile into never bothering him again.

Color Changers

Celebrating Me

I am the only ME I AM who qualifies as me;
No ME I AM has been before, and none will ever be.

No other ME I AM can feel the feelings I've within;
No other ME I AM can fit precisely in my skin.

There is no other ME I AM who thinks the thoughts I do;
The world contains one ME I AM, there is no room for two.

I am the only ME I AM this earth shall ever see;
That ME I AM I always am is no one else but ME!

—Anonymous

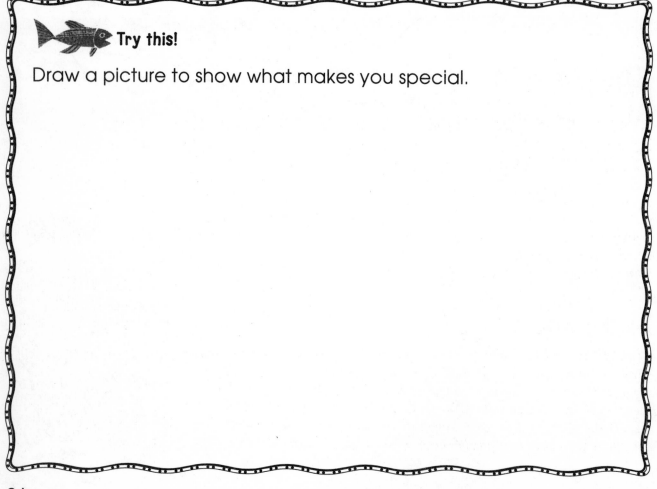

Try this!

Draw a picture to show what makes you special.

The Grouchy Ladybug

(HarperCollins, 1977)

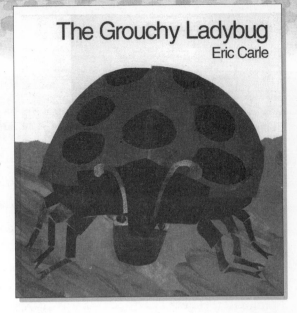

The Grouchy Ladybug
Eric Carle

A bad-tempered ladybug and a friendly ladybug spot an aphid-covered leaf at the same time. The friendly ladybug offers to share. The grouchy ladybug picks a fight with her instead, then goes off to pick fights with a dozen other creatures, each one bigger than the one before. The last one, a whale, sends the ladybug back to the leaf with a flick of its tail, where a lesson on friendship and manners awaits.

BEFORE READING

Cranky, Crabby, and Other Words for Grouchy

Grouchy—it's a word we could all use to describe our feelings at one time or another. Invite students to tell what they think this word means. Record their ideas on chart paper. Discuss other words with a similar meaning, such as *cranky*, *crabby*, and *irritable*. (See "A Word Wall of Feelings," page 29, for a related activity.) Ask: *What kinds of things make you grouchy? Why do you think the ladybug in the story is grouchy?*

Eating Aphids

As your students will learn in this story, ladybugs enjoy eating aphids. But what are these tasty treats? Familiarize your students with these tiny creatures before reading the story by sharing the science background in the front of the 1996 edition of *The Grouchy Ladybug*. (*Aphids are tiny bugs that eat leaves, harming the plants in the process. Ladybugs are helpful bugs to have in a garden because they like to eat the aphids!*)

CONCEPTS and THEMES
- feelings
- conflict resolution
- size

Word Play

Reread the story, asking children to listen for the lines that repeat as the grouchy ladybug encounters each new animal: ("Hey you...want to fight?" "If you insist." "Oh, you're not big enough...") Ask students what they notice about the word you're. Draw their attention to the apostrophe. Explain that words like this are called contractions. When two words are shortened to make one, the apostrophe takes the place of the missing letter or letters. Ask: *Do you know what two words were shortened to make the word you're?* (you and are) *What letter does the apostrophe take the place of?* (a) Let students go through the book and find other contractions, then take turns writing the words on the chalkboard, along with the two words that make each contraction.

Book Talk

Use these questions to spark a discussion about the story.

⭐ How was the ladybug feeling at the beginning and middle of the story? How does this compare with how she was feeling at the end?

⭐ Why do you think the ladybug picked fights with the other animals? What are some things you do when you're grouchy?

⭐ If you were the ladybug's friend, what would you say to her about picking fights? What are some other ways to handle a bad mood?

⭐ What do you think the ladybug learned at the end of the story?

LANGUAGE ARTS
Compound Word Puzzles

Use the title to introduce compound words. Read the title aloud and write it on the chalkboard. Ask: *Which word is made by putting two words together?* (ladybug) Explain that words that are made by putting two words together are called *compound words*. Let students share other compound words they know, such as *doghouse* and *firetruck*. Write the words on the board, and let children underline the two words that combine to make each compound word. Reinforce students' understanding by letting them build more compound words. Give each child a copy of page 31. Have children color and cut out the word puzzles on the dashed lines. Ask children to mix up their puzzle pieces, then put them back together to make compound words.

MATH
Ladybug Time

Give each child a copy of the clock template on page 32. Guide children in putting their clocks together, using a paper fastener to attach the minute and hour hands. Reread the story, letting children use their clocks to show the time of each of the ladybug's encounters. Let children use their clocks as props in their own retellings of the story.

A Word Wall of Feelings

Word walls strengthen reading and writing skills, making a quick and easy resource for children who are searching for exactly the right word—or just the spelling. A word wall of feelings will also extend students' vocabulary, giving them language for their feelings that is more precise than the frequently used *happy, sad,* and *mad.*

Review words that have a meaning similar to *grouchy.* (See "*Cranky, Crabby,* and Other Words for *Grouchy,*" page 27.) Ask: *What are some other words for feelings we have?* Supply students with paper plates, crayons or markers, yarn, and other art materials. Invite children to choose a feeling from the list and draw a face that shows this feeling. Have them write the words for the feeling at the bottom of the plate. Display the paper plates on a wall. Let students add to it as they discover new words for feelings. Be sure to revisit the word wall regularly, letting children read the words. For a variation, let them sort the plates—for example, grouping together plates with words that are similar to *happy.*

MATH, SCIENCE

Symmetrical Spots Collaborative Banner

Ask students to take a close look at the ladybug in the book. Have them count the spots on each wing. Ask: *What do you notice about the ladybug's spots?* (There are the same number of spots on each wing.) Introduce the word *symmetrical.* Explain that a ladybug's wings are symmetrical because the spots are the same on each side. Invite children to notice ways that their own bodies are symmetrical—for example, they have an ear on each side of their head, and an eye on each side of their nose. Make a collaborative banner to explore a ladybug's symmetry—and the math skill of doubling numbers.

✭ Give each child a copy of page 33. Have children color in spots on one of the ladybug's wings, then fold the paper in half and trace the spots on the other side. Children can then unfold their papers and use the traced lines to make symmetrical spots on the other wing.

✭ Have children complete the number sentences to show how many spots their ladybugs have.

✭ Have children glue or tape their ladybugs in a line on a sheet of craft paper. Display the banner at children's eye level.

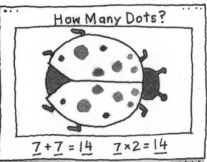

How Many Dots?

$7 + 7 = 14$ $7 \times 2 = 14$

Share this rhyme about ladybugs. Then reread it and invite students to move about like the ladybugs.

LADYBUG RHYME

Ladybugs all dressed in red

Strolling through the flower bed—

If I were tiny just like you,

I'd creep among the flowers, too.

—Maria Fleming

SCIENCE
Ladybug Life Cycles

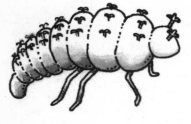

Many animal babies look like their parents—smaller, with slightly different features, but quite similar. Other baby animals look very different from their parents. These babies change as they grow, eventually reaching the adult stage of their life cycle in which they look like their parents. Ask your students if they know what a baby ladybug looks like. *(The ladybug larva looks more like an ant than a ladybug;* see illustration, left.) Let students investigate the life cycle of a ladybug. Some questions to answer include:

★ What does a baby ladybug look like?

★ In what ways does the ladybug change as it grows?

★ Does a ladybug undergo metamorphosis?

MATH
How Many Aphids Can a Ladybug Eat?

Ladybug beetles eat aphids. Ladybug larvae like aphids, too! How many might they munch on in a day? Let your students estimate, then count to find out. Count out 500 small objects—such as uncooked rice or small noodles—to represent aphids. Cut large leaf shapes out of green paper. Scatter the "aphids" on the leaves. Ask: *How many aphids do you think are on these leaves?* Record guesses, then have children group the aphids by tens. Count together by tens to find out how many aphids were on the leaves. That's how many the larvae of some ladybug species can eat in just one day!

LEARN MORE

Books

The Ladybug and Other Insects by Pascale de Bourgoing (Scholastic, 1991). Peek through the transparent pages of this colorful book to explore the life cycle of a ladybug.

A Ladybug's Life by John Himmelman (Children's Press, 1998). A big, bright ladybug invites readers inside to learn more.

Web Sites

Canadian Nature Federation (**www.cnf.ca**): What's the difference between a Nine-Spotted Lady Beetle and a Hieroglyphic Lady Beetle? Click on pictures of more than a dozen ladybugs to get identifying characteristics and close-up photos.

Other

Ladybug Lodge (Insect Lore, phone 800-LIVEBUG). This activity kit includes a mail-in certificate for 75 to 100 ladybugs.

Compound Word Puzzles

lady bug

bird house

bed room

book shelf

birth day

air plane

tree house

snow flake

Ladybug Time

Name _____

How Many Dots?

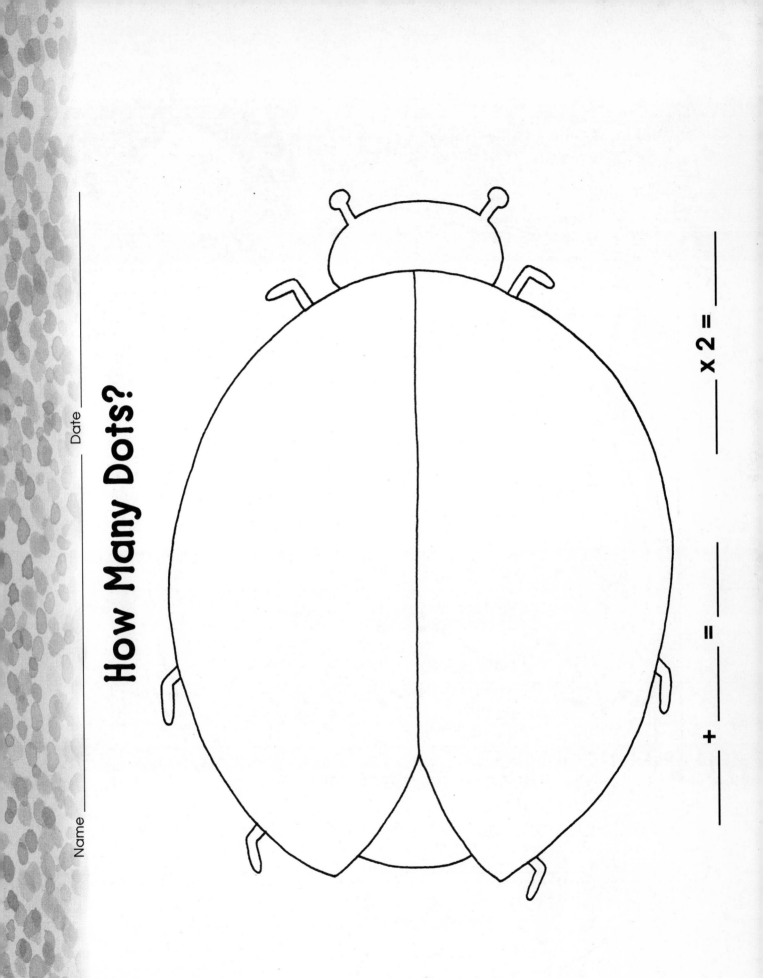

___ + ___ = ___ x 2 = ___

The Tiny Seed

(Simon & Schuster, 1987)

A tiny seed travels from one place to another, eventually settling in the earth, where a winter snow covers it until spring. Sun and rain help the seed grow, and by late summer it is a giant flower. When autumn comes along, the flower's petals drop, the wind shakes the seed pod open, and the seeds sail away, bringing the story right back to the beginning.

BEFORE READING

Seed Size

Let students share what they know about seeds. Bring in some seeds so that students can better picture the tiny seed in the story as it's blown about in the wind.

Naming the Seasons

The seasons are an important part of this story. Help children focus on the significance of each season in the story by reviewing names of the seasons and what they know about each. This will give children a framework for listening when you share the story.

CONCEPTS and THEMES
- nature
- plants and seeds
- seasons

Book Talk

After sharing the story, ask: *What do you think would happen next in the story if the author kept going?* Guide children to recognize that the story follows the seasons in a cyclical order. They'll recognize a beginning in the ending—it's autumn once again, and the seeds are sailing away with the wind. Review the names of the seasons. Ask: *What season is it now? What season came before this one? What season will come next?*

SCIENCE

Traveling Seeds

Give each child several popcorn kernels. Review some of the ways seeds travel. Let students experiment with ways to make their seeds travel. For example, how can they make them sticky, like seeds with burrs? Will their seeds float on water?

Conclude by asking students why it is important for seeds to move from one place to another. (*If seeds stayed with the parent plant, the new plants would compete for nutrients, soil, water, and sunlight. Overcrowding could result in the plants being unable to survive.*)

LANGUAGE ARTS

A Tiny Word Wall

Ask students why they think the author used the word *tiny* to describe the seed. Brainstorm other words with a similar meaning—for example, *small, little, miniature,* and *petite.* Try out each of these words in the title, in place of the word *tiny.* Which do they like best? Record synonyms for *tiny* on flower-shaped cutouts, and display. Let children add to the wall with new words they find.

LANGUAGE ARTS, SCIENCE

Make a Story Circle

Bring out the cyclical structure of *The Tiny Seed* by making a story circle. Draw a large circle on chart paper. Label the seasons as shown (*winter, spring, summer, fall*). Ask students to retell the story, using the seasons as a guide to sequence the events. Record their retelling on the circle, moving from winter to spring, summer, and fall. Share another story with a cyclical structure, such as *This Quiet Lady* by Charlotte Zolotow (Greenwillow, 1992). Have children retell the story on their own story circles.

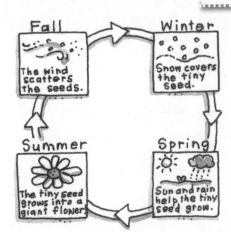

POETRY BREAK

Introduce an investigation of the ways seeds travel with "Yellow Weed," by Lilian Moore. (See page 37.) Before sharing the poem, ask students how they think seeds get from one place to another—for example:

- Some seeds are carried by the wind.
- Some seeds have barbs or hooks that can catch a ride on people or animals.
- Some seeds travel on bodies of water.
- Some seeds are moved by animals that eat them. For example, squirrels gather acorns, moving them from the places they drop to new places. Some are eaten. Others get forgotten and are left to grow into new trees.

Sprout Like a Seed

Sprout some real seeds in the classroom (dried lima beans sprout in just a few days), then review steps in the growing process. (*A seed is planted and kept moist. It germinates, or sprouts, then continues to grow with water and sunlight.*) Invite children to show what they know about how seeds grow with a guided imagery activity. Ask them to imagine they are seeds being planted in the ground. Continue to describe what happens with descriptive words (*the farmer is sprinkling water on you, the sun warms you,* etc.). Have them move like a seed—sprouting and growing until they are reaching for the sky.

Word Play

Let children look back through the story for words and phrases the author uses to paint pictures of each season—for example, *sun, snow, rain, petals drop, leaves are bright,* and *plants grow.* Ask: *What season are we in now?* Let children use words from the story, as well as other words, to write sentences about the current season. Have them draw pictures of what they think the tiny seed would be doing where they live (*blowing about, germinating, growing tall,* and so on).

MATH
A Garden of Patterns

The flowers on page 38 are growing in patterns. Give each child a copy of the pattern page and some crayons. Have children follow the directions to grow a garden. Follow up by placing a flower guide book (see Learn More, below), large sheets of paper, and crayons or markers at a learning center. Let children use the guide book and other materials to start new flower patterns. Display the patterns for other students to continue.

🐞 LEARN MORE

Books

National Audubon Society First Field Guide: Wildflowers (Scholastic, 1998). This easy-to-use guide contains facts, photographs, and illustrations for more than 150 flowers, including 50 in North America.

I'm a Seed by Jean Marzollo (Scholastic, 1996). This Hello Reader! book invites young readers to follow along as two seeds take root and grow. One stem grows up. One stem grows sideways!

Ride the Wind: Airborne Journeys of Animals and Plants by Seymour Simon (Harcourt Brace, 1997). Travel along with plants and animals as they sail away with the wind.

Web Sites

National Gardening Association (**www.kids gardening.com**): Check here for gardening activities, classroom stories, partner projects, garden grants, and lots more.

Did You Know (**www.didyouknow.com/flowers. htm**): What's the biggest flower in the world? Find the answer here!

Yellow Weed

How did you get here,
weed?
Who brought your seed?

Did it lift
on the wind and
sail
and drift
from a far and yellow
field?

Was your seed a
burr,
a sticky burr that
clung to a
fox's
furry tail?

Did it fly with a
bird
who liked to feed
on the tasty
seed
of the yellow
weed?

How did you come?

—Lilian Moore

A Garden of Patterns

- ◎ Cut out each strip of flowers.
- ◎ Glue the strips on paper.
- ◎ Look at the flowers in each row. Do you see a pattern?
- ◎ Draw what comes next in the pattern. Color your flowers!

Teaching With Favorite Eric Carle Books Scholastic Professional Books

The Very Busy Spider

(Philomel, 1984)

A little spider begins to spin a web. Diligent spider that she is, she resists the distractions of a horse, cow, sheep, and a half dozen other animals as she weaves and weaves. The story's rhythmic language lulls unsuspecting readers as the web grows page by page, until "just like that!" she catches a fly.

BEFORE READING

Web Builders

Invite students to make predictions about the busy spider. Ask: *Why do you think the spider in this book is so busy?* Encourage children to explain the reasons behind their ideas.

All About Bugs

Invite students to share what they know about spiders. Let them tell what they know about insects, too. Ask: *How are spiders like insects you know? How are they different?*

CONCEPTS and THEMES
- diligence
- farm life
- predator/prey
- habitats

Book Talk

The rhythmic language of this story is mesmerizing—right up to the end when readers are jolted by the fly getting caught in the spider's web. Invite children to respond to the ending. Were they surprised? Ask them to share reactions to the pages leading up to the ending, too.

LANGUAGE ARTS

Barnyard Sounds

The animals in *The Very Busy Spider* speak up, trying to talk the spider into running in the meadow, chasing cats, and more. Reread the story, letting children chime in on the animal sounds (*Baa, baa!, Neigh, neigh!,* and so on.) Then play a barnyard game that lets students have fun with the sounds while strengthening listening skills.

⭐ Make game cards for each child by gluing pictures of animals from the story, and other barnyard animals, on index cards. (See animal pictures, pages 42–43.) Make sets of cards, so that each animal has a matching card (two sheep cards, two horse cards, two dog cards, and so on).

⭐ Punch holes in the top left and right corners of the cards. String with yarn to make necklaces. Give each child a necklace. Have children color their cards, then put their necklaces on <u>picture-side down</u>.

⭐ Explain to children that they need to find the classmate who has a matching card. They can do this by moving about the room, making the sound their animal makes. They will also need to listen to the sounds around them to find their matches.

⭐ Have children who think they have found a match sit down together and turn their necklaces picture-side out. When everyone has found a match, invite children to share what they know about their animals—for example, what they like to eat.

LANGUAGE ARTS

Who Said That?

Introduce quotation marks using the dialogue from the story. Begin by writing a sentence from the story on the chalkboard—for example, *"Baa! Baa!" bleated the sheep. "Want to run in the meadow?"* Ask: *Who said "Baa! Baa!" ?* (the sheep) Explain that the quotation marks tell exactly what the animal said. Let students find other quotation marks in the book. Guide them to understand that the quotation marks go both before and after what the animal said. Let students practice using quotation marks by pairing up and recording sentences that the other says.

Word Play

Revisit the story, letting children look for animal names, including:

   horse
   cow
   sheep
   goat
   dog
   cat
   pig
   duck
   rooster
   owl

Follow up by having children name as many other animals as they can that might live on a farm. Record the words on chart paper or the chalkboard. (For a related activity, see "Barnyard Sounds," right.)

LANGUAGE ARTS
Perform a Mini-Play

Turn your classroom into a lively barnyard with a dramatic reading of the story. Divide the class into ten groups—one for each animal part and one for the narrator's repeating response. (*"The spider didn't answer. She was very busy spinning her web."*) Let groups practice their lines, then bring them together to reread the story.

LANGUAGE ARTS
Tell a New Story

This story lends itself to a retelling, with children replacing the existing animals with others. Start by asking children to think of other animals, the sounds they make, and the things they might ask the spider to do. Have children write and illustrate sentences, using the dialogue in the book as a model—for example, *"Chirp! Chirp!" said the bird. "Want to catch worms?"* Retell the story, letting children take turns substituting their sentences for the ones in the book.

SCIENCE
Spider Fact Fun

How fast do spiders spin? Do all spiders spin webs? Conduct a class research project to investigate children's questions about spiders. Write and display facts on spider-shaped cards.

 **Tip**

To do more with performing arts, make a class set of the animal cards on pages 42–43. Let children color in and cut out the animals, then glue them to craft sticks. Children can use the puppets to retell the story on their own or with a small group.

Tip

Students may be surprised to learn that horseshoe crabs are members of the same group as spiders. They are arachnids! Other members of this group include scorpions, mites, and ticks.

🕷 LEARN MORE

Books

Anansi the Spider: A Tale From the Ashanti by Gerald McDermott (Henry Holt, 1973). This Caldecott Honor winner tells the tale of Anansi the hero-spider and how his six sons work together to save him.

Dream Weaver by Jonathan London (Harcourt Brace, 1998). "Nestled in the soft earth beside the path, you see a little yellow spider…" Simple text and radiant illustrations tell a magical nighttime story of a spider spinning her web. The last page includes a list of fascinating spider facts.

Miss Spider's Tea Party by David Kirk (Scholastic, 1994). Who will join Miss Spider for tea? Fireflies, ants, and other creatures all refuse—fearing they'll be Miss Spider's snack instead. Then one little moth accepts and makes it out alive—paving the way for more new friends for the spider. Rhyming text and awesome art make the book a favorite.

National Audubon Society Field Guide to North American Insects and Spiders by Lorus J. Milne (Knopf, 1995). Photos of 60 kinds of spiders, plus descriptive text. Includes measurements, what they eat, web construction, folklore, and more.

Spiders by Rhonda Lucas Donald and Kathleen W. Kranking (Scholastic Professional Books, 1999). This theme unit includes hands-on activities, plus a big colorful poster.

Web Sites

Arachnology Home Page (**www.ufsia.ac.be/ Arachnology/Pages/Kids.html**): Download a spider screensaver, then get answers to all sorts of spider questions, including "Why doesn't a spider get stuck in its own web?"

Barnyard Sounds

Teaching With Favorite Eric Carle Books Scholastic Professional Books

Barnyard Sounds

Papa, Please Get the Moon for Me

(Simon & Schuster, 1986)

This inviting story unfolds—with pages that open up, out, and down—to tell about a young girl who is determined to play with the moon. She can't reach it, so she asks her papa to get it for her. He climbs a very long ladder to the moon, but it is too big to carry down. Soon, though, it grows smaller and smaller, until at last he can carry it down. His daughter plays and dances with the moon, until it disappears. It reappears in the sky as a sliver and grows bigger and bigger each night.

CONCEPTS and THEMES
- © moon phases
- © size
- © patterns

BEFORE READING

Fiction or Nonfiction?

After sharing the title, ask: *Do you think someone could really get the moon?* Discuss what kind of a story this is. *(fiction)* Let students point out other examples of fiction books in the classroom. Review the difference between fiction and nonfiction. Invite students to point out examples of nonfiction, too.

Reach for the Moon

Give students a good stretch before settling down to hear this story by inviting them to "reach for the moon" as the young girl in the story does. You might suspend a large full-moon shape from the ceiling first. Let students reach and reach, then read the story.

Book Talk

Your students will delight in the foldout pages of *Papa, Please Get the Moon for Me*. Revisit the foldout pages. Ask: *Why do you think the illustrator wanted these pages to fold out?* (For example, one foldout helps readers feel how high the moon is; another helps us feel how big the moon is.)

LANGUAGE ARTS, SCIENCE

Story Patterns

Give each child a copy of the patterns on page 48. Let children color in the patterns and cut them out, then glue them to craft sticks to make puppets. Have them use their puppets to retell the story. Before they begin, talk about the order of the moon phases in the book. Let children arrange their moon cutouts in the order they think matches the order in the book. Revisit the pictures in the book to check the order. Ask: *What phase was the moon at the beginning of the story?* (See the four-page foldout picturing the full moon.) *What phases did the moon go through as it got smaller and smaller? What phase was the moon when it disappeared? What phase was the moon at the end of the story?* Store the patterns in resealable sandwich bags, and let children take them home to retell the story for their families.

ART, SCIENCE

My Favorite Moon

Eric Carle's enchanting collage illustrations light up the night sky. Ask students to decide on a favorite moon phase illustration from the book. Then have them create their own illustrations of the moon using collage. Provide tissue paper in assorted colors, drawing paper, glitter, white glue thinned with water, paintbrushes, and scissors. Let children first arrange torn-and-cut tissue paper to represent the moon in their favorite phases. When they are satisfied with the placement, have them glue the tissue paper in place, layer by layer. When the collage is complete, they can paint a top layer of glue over the entire surface, then sprinkle on glitter. Let the artwork dry, then display.

Word Play

Which words in the story tell what the characters did? Write the first two sentences of the story on the chalkboard: "Before Monica went to bed she looked out of her window and saw the moon. The moon looked so near." Ask children to find the word in the sentence that tells what the girl did. (*looked*) Guide children in finding the little word in *looked*. (*look*) Ask: Why did the author add -ed to the word look? Introduce -ed endings. Then challenge children to find other words in the story that describe what characters did, including:

stretched
reached
carried
climbed
jumped
danced
hugged
disappeared

 **Tip**

For more information about the Native American moons, see *Twelve Moons of the Year* by Hal Borland (G.K. Hall, 1985), a collection of nature essays.

POETRY BREAK

Share a poem about the moon. (See below.) Ask: *What phase of the moon is the poet describing?* (crescent) Let children illustrate themselves looking up at the night sky, using information from the newspaper or an almanac to show what phase the moon is in. Have them write poems or sentences describing the moon in their pictures.

WINTER MOON
How thin and sharp is the moon tonight!
How thin and sharp and ghostly white
Is the slim curved crook of the moon tonight!
—Langston Hughes

SCIENCE, SOCIAL STUDIES
Native American Moons

Explain to students that hundreds of years ago, Native Americans gave the moon for each month a name. The names were based on weather or natural events. Share the Native American name for the moon for the current month. (See below.) Ask students: *Why do you think people gave the moon this name?* Let students share their ideas. Follow up by explaining the meaning behind each month's moon name. Let children write and illustrate a collaborative book about the Native American moon names.

As an extension, let students team up to give the moon for each month a *new* name. Give each team a month. Have students discuss seasonal characteristics of the month and possible names, then vote on one. Bring students together to share the new moon names and their reasons for choosing those names.

January: Wolf Moon (for the time when the "fangs" of winter bite and the wind howls)

February: Snow Moon (for the time when the ground is covered with deep snow)

March: Worm Moon (for the time when worms make their way through ground that is thawing)

April: Pink Moon (for the first spring flowers)

May: Flower Moon (another reference to spring flowers)

June: Hot Moon (for the heat of summer and summer solstice)

July: Buck Moon (a time to dry meats in the summer heat)

August: Green Corn Moon (corn is ripening)

September: Harvest Moon (for the full moon that provides farmers with extra light for harvesting crops)

October: Hunter's Moon (for a moon that gives light for hunting)

November: Beaver Moon (a time for hunting and, like the wise beaver, providing for winter)

December: Cold Moon (for the longest nights of the year and winter solstice)

SCIENCE, LANGUAGE ARTS
Make a Moon Banner

Display a banner-size sheet of paper on a wall. Divide the banner into sections, one for each day of the month. Each day, have a different child report on the shape of the moon the previous night. (This information can be gathered through observation or by checking a newspaper or almanac.) Have this child draw a picture of the moon on the banner with white crayon. Repeat this for each day of the month, filling in weekend moons on Mondays. When the banner is complete, let children paint the banner black. The moon shapes colored with white crayon will resist the paint, creating a night sky effect. Provide a star-like sparkle by sprinkling glitter around the moon shapes. Finally, have students identify each phase of the moon and label the pictures.

SCIENCE AND SNACK
Munching on the Moon ....

Share a snack that students can nibble to show the phases of the moon as they appear in the story. Give each child a round sugar cookie or large, round cracker. Ask children to name the phase of the moon that looks most like the cookie or cracker before they eat it. (*full*) Review the order of the phases of the moon from largest to smallest: *full, gibbous, quarter, crescent, new.* Reread the story, letting children nibble on their cookies each time the moon enters a new phase. When the cookies are finished, ask: *What phase is the moon in now?* (new—not visible) *How is the real moon in this phase different from your cookies?* (It does not really disappear.)

....

LEARN MORE

Books

National Audobon Society First Field Guide: Night Sky (Scholastic, 1999). Easy-to-read text, maps, and more make this a great guide for beginners.

The Moon Seems to Change by Franklyn Branley (HarperTrophy, 1987). This Let's-Read-and-Find-Out book features a simple experiment that lets children find out why the moon looks different at different times of the month.

What the Moon Is Like by Franklyn Branley (HarperTrophy, 1986). NASA photos and information gathered by Apollo space missions enhance this Let's-Read-and-Find-Out book.

Where Does the Moon Go? by Sidney Rosen (Carolrhoda, 1992). Striking photographs and clear illustrations help explain the phases of the moon.

Web Sites

Try these web sites for more information about the phases of the moon, including facts, photos, and lots of links.

aa.usno.navy.mil/AA/data/

www.solarviews.com/eng/moon.htm

seds.lpl.arizona.edu/nineplanets/ nineplanets/luna.html

www.enchantedlearning.com/subjects/ astronomy/moon/index/shtml

Story Patterns

A House for Hermit Crab

(Simon & Schuster, 1987)

Hermit Crab has outgrown his shell and must look for a new home. He finds a big, strong house to move into, but misses the homeyness of his old shell. One by one, he finds sea creatures to transform the plain shell into a place that feels like home. And when that shell's too small? Along comes a smaller crab who will feel right at home with Hermit Crab's friends.

CONCEPTS and THEMES
- homes and habitats
- sea life
- friendship

BEFORE READING

Sea Words

Ask students to name things that live in the sea. Ask: *Which of these things do you think we'll read about in this story?* Write the words on chart paper and display. Encourage students to listen for words in the story that name sea creatures.

What We Know

Ask students to share information about hermit crabs. For example, they might know that they live in the shells of other animals, such as snails. Record students' comments on chart paper labeled "What We Know." Ask students what they would like to learn about hermit crabs. Record their questions on a second sheet of chart paper labeled "What We Want to Know." After sharing the story, see "All About Hermit Crabs" (page 50) to learn more.

Word Play

Let students revisit the story to see if any of the words on their list (see "Sea Words," page 49) match words for creatures in the story. These include:

- sea anemones
- starfish
- corals
- snails
- sea urchins
- lantern fish

Use the glossary in the back of *A House for Hermit Crab* to learn more about each creature.

Book Talk

What makes a house a home? Ask children to answer this question for Hermit Crab. Discuss what they think will happen when he finds his next home. Ask: *Have you ever moved to a new home? What did you miss about your old home? What are some things you did to feel better about your new home? What makes the place where you live "home"?*

LANGUAGE ARTS, SCIENCE
Puppet Play

Give each child a copy of page 51. Have children color and cut out the patterns and glue them to craft sticks. Invite children to use the puppets to retell the story in their own words and to make up new stories about the characters in *A House for Hermit Crab*.

LANGUAGE ARTS
Consonant Blend Word-Builders

Use the word *crab* as a springboard to learning more about the consonant blend /cr/. Write the word *crab* on one of the crab-shaped cutouts. (See page 51.) Ask students to make the sound for the first two letters. (*cr*) Explain that these two letters combine to make one sound. Ask students if they can think of other words that have the same beginning sound as *crab*—for example, *cream, crumb, create, croak, creak,* and *cry*. Write these words on crab-shaped cutouts and read them together. Display the words on a wall. Revisit them regularly, rereading the words and adding new words.

LEARN MORE

Books

The Aquarium Take-Along Book by Sheldon L. Gerstenfeld, V.M.D. (Penguin, 1994). Learn all about the marine world with this fun-filled guidebook.

The Classroom Pet (First Grade Friends, Hello Reader) by Grace Maccarone (Scholastic, 1995). The unthinkable happens to first-grader Sam—he accidentally loses the class pet, a hermit crab.

The Crab Man by Van West (Turtle Books, 1998). This book will inspire discussion among your students as they contemplate the choice of a young Jamaican boy who finds out the hermit crabs he sells are being treated cruelly.

One Small Square: Seashore by Donald M. Silver (Freeman, 1993). Take a close look at a variety of creatures that make their home at the seashore.

Web Sites

Zooish (**www.zooish.com**): See animals come to life at this kid-friendly place.

The Complete Online Hermit Crab Guide (**hermitcrabs.cjb.net/**): Learn about a hermit crab's habitat, behavior, feeding habits, and more.

Puppet Play Patterns

Today Is Monday

(Putnam, 1993)

Colorful collages bring food and animals to life in this picture-book version of the well-known children's song. Each day of the week features an animal enjoying a different food, ending with a culinary feast for all the hungry children. Cumulative text makes this a good choice for beginning readers, who will enjoy chiming in as each food is repeated from one day to the next.

CONCEPTS and THEMES
- ◎ days of the week
- ◎ counting
- ◎ nutrition

BEFORE READING

Funny Pet Stories

Share the cover of the book. Ask children what animal they see pictured. (*a cat*) Ask: *What's unusual about this cat?* (It's wearing a bib and is holding a fork and a knife.) Give children a few minutes to share their own funny pet stories.

Today Is...

Introduce the story by writing this sentence on the chalkboard: *Today is _____ .* Let children complete the sentence any way they like. (*Today is [day of the week], [Henry's birthday], [gym day],* etc.) Read the title of the book, then share names for other days of the week. Write these on the board, and ask children to listen for them as you read the story.

Book Talk

After sharing the story, invite children to tell what their favorite food of the week was: *string beans, spaghetti, soup, roast beef, fresh fish, chicken,* or *ice cream.* What seven foods would children include if they were telling the story? (For a related activity, see "Make a Mini-Book," below.)

SOCIAL STUDIES, LANGUAGE ARTS

Days-of-the-Week Story Map

Reinforce the names of the days of the week, and children's ability to retell stories, by making a story map of *Today Is Monday.* Display a length of craft paper. Divide it into seven sections, one for each day of the week. Write the names for the days of the week at the top of each section. Reread the story, asking children to listen carefully for the names of the days of the week and the foods for each. Ask children to recall the food for each day, and record it on the story map. Let children illustrate each food, then use the story map as a guide to retell the story to one another.

LANGUAGE ARTS

Make a Mini-Book

Use the book as inspiration for children's own stories about the days of the week.

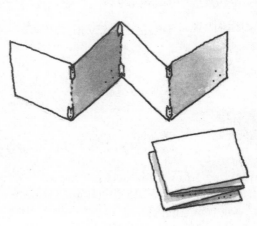

- ⭐ Make a blank accordion-fold book for each child by taping four sheets of paper together end to end. Fold each page back and forth accordion-style, as shown.

- ⭐ Have children use the page on top to make a cover. On each additional page, have children complete and illustrate these sentence frames: *Today is [day of the week]. [Day of the week] is [food].*

MATH

Set the Table for Math

Learn more about the days of the week with an activity that introduces ordinal numbers.

- ⭐ Begin by looking at a calendar. Ask children which day of the week is listed first. (*Sunday*) Explain that this is the *first day* of the week.

- ⭐ Write the words *Sunday* and *first* on dessert-size paper plates. Let children name the other days of the week in order. Give the ordinal number for each in turn. Write these on paper plates, too.

Tip

Make a math connection by graphing children's choices for favorite foods in the story. Ask them first to predict which food will get the most votes.

Word Play

Ask students if they notice anything special about the word Monday. (It starts with a capital letter.) Look for other words in the story with capital letters. Write these words on the chalkboard and group them—for example, by days of the week . Help students see that some of the words are capitalized because they are names for things (*proper nouns*). Others are capital because they start sentences.

★ Revisit the story and let children name the food for each day of the week. Draw pictures (or cut them from magazines) of each food (*ice cream*, *string beans*, *spaghetti*, *soup*, *roast beef*, *fish*, *chicken*) and glue these to paper plates.

★ Display the plates (days of the week, ordinal numbers, pictures) at a learning center. Let children work with partners to match the plates at the table. For an extra touch, place a tablecloth on the table and set out plastic forks and spoons. Children can set the table with the paper plates, arranging them around the table in order.

SCIENCE
Today's Weather

Reinforce vocabulary for the names of the days of the week with a daily weather graph. Give each child a copy of the weather graph. (See page 55.) Each day, have students complete the sentence by filling in the day and the appropriate weather word(s). Have children color in a picture on the graph to show the day's weather. Let children take turns reading their sentences aloud—for example, *Today is Monday. Monday is partly sunny.* At the end of the week, guide a discussion of the data children have collected—for example, ask:

★ Was the weather this week mostly sunny, partly sunny, cloudy, rainy, or snowy?

★ Did we have more [weather condition] or [weather condition] days?

★ How many more [weather condition] days did we have than [weather condition] days?

LEARN MORE

Books

All in a Day by Mitsumasa Anno et alia (Philomel, 1986). Eric Carle is among the notable contributors to an informative book that treats readers to a colorful journey around the world to see what's happening in a moment in time. While some are sleeping, others are playing. While there's snow for some, it's a warm day at the beach for others.

Day by Day a Week Goes Round by Carol Diggory Shields (Dutton, 1998). This bright book uses rhyming text to introduce the names of the days of the week. Children will also gain an appreciation for what makes each day special.

Web Sites

Today in History (**www.learningkingdom.com**): See what made the news each day with Today in History. (You can sign up to have it e-mailed to you.) You can also make Person of the Day, Cool Fact of the Day, and Cool Word of the Day part of your daily routine.

Today's Weather

Complete the sentence to tell what the weather is each day. Color a picture on the graph to show what the weather is each day.

Today is _____. _____ is _____.
      (day)   (day)   (weather)

Today is _____. _____ is _____.
      (day)   (day)   (weather)

Today is _____. _____ is _____.
      (day)   (day)   (weather)

Today is _____. _____ is _____.
      (day)   (day)   (weather)

Today is _____. _____ is _____.
      (day)   (day)   (weather)

sunny	**partly sunny**	**cloudy**	**rainy**	**snowy**

Eric Carle   The Very Lonely Firefly

The Very Lonely Firefly

(Philomel, 1995)

Messages of love and belonging are woven into this story of a firefly seeking a family. The firefly goes from one place to another, flashing its light in search of other fireflies. Time after time, the firefly finds that the light it flies toward belongs to something else—a lightbulb, a candle, a flashlight, a lantern, a dog and cat, headlights, even fireworks. But perseverance pays off—the firefly finally finds a family.

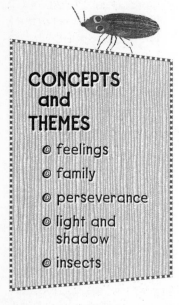

CONCEPTS and THEMES

- ◎ feelings
- ◎ family
- ◎ perseverance
- ◎ light and shadow
- ◎ insects

BEFORE READING

Lights On!

How many of your students have seen fireflies? Ask: *When do they light up?* Introduce the word *nocturnal.* Explain that fireflies are nocturnal—they come out at night. Invite children to tell what they think the illustrations in the story will be like. (*They're nighttime scenes.*) There's a surprise waiting for them at the end—a page of blinking fireflies lights up the night sky! (For a related activity, see page 58.)

Insects We Know

Ask students what group of animals they think fireflies belong to. (*insects*) Let them share what they know about insects. Invite students to look at the firefly on the cover. Ask: *What body parts tell you a firefly is an insect?* (It has six legs, three body parts, and so on.)

Book Talk

Like many of the characters in Eric Carle's books, the firefly in this story has feelings and experiences that young children can learn from. Ask your students about the firefly's feelings and what it means to be lonely. Let children share times they've felt lonely. Perhaps there are days when they can't find a friend to play with on the playground. Talk about how the firefly felt at the end of the story. Discuss the idea of *belonging*. What helps children feel a sense of belonging? What can they do to help others feel the same?

LANGUAGE ARTS
Word-Builders Memory Game

Make copies of the compound word cards on page 59, filling in the blank cards with words of your choice. Let children color and cut out the cards, then follow these directions to play a matching game in small groups.

* Mix up the cards and place them facedown.

* Take turns selecting two cards. If the words can make a compound word together, keep them. If not, place the cards facedown again.

* Continue playing until all the matches are made.

* Provide children with blank cards. Let them make new Word-Builders Memory Games with other compound words.

SCIENCE
A Firefly's Family

Students may be surprised to learn that fireflies are not flies at all! They are part of the beetle family. Science notes in the front of *The Very Lonely Firefly* give additional background information on fireflies. Let students prepare a presentation on fireflies. Have them research additional facts and record them on firefly-shaped cards. Display the cards on a wall, then darken the room, and let children use a flashlight to illuminate their fact cards and read them aloud.

MATH, MOVEMENT
Counting Fireflies

In *Ten Flashing Fireflies* by Philemon Sturges (North South Books, 1995), a young boy and girl capture ten fireflies, one by one, and place them in a jar. As each firefly's light disappears from the sky, it reappears in the jar, until there are ten fireflies all together. The book concludes with the fireflies being released from the jar, first one, then another, until one by one they all fly away. Practice addition and subtraction by letting children act out the story. Give each of ten children a flashlight. Dim the room as you read the

Word Play

Write the word firefly on the chalkboard. Ask: *What two words do you see in this word?* (fire, fly) Let children revisit the story to look for compound words, including the following:

> firefly
> lightbulb
> flashlight
> headlight
> fireworks

Write the words on the board, and let volunteers identify the two words that make up each word. Together, brainstorm other compound words. (See "Word-Builders Memory Game," left, for a related activity.)

 Tip

Some students might know fireflies by another name—lightning bugs! The larvae of fireflies are called *glowworms*.

story. Let the children flash their lights to show what happens in the story, grouping together as they are placed in the jar, and "flying away" as they are released. Reread the story several times to give each child a chance to be a firefly.

SCIENCE
Closeup on a Firefly

Let children take a close-up look at a picture of a firefly to learn about its parts. Start by displaying a large picture of a firefly. Write each insect part on an index card and display around the firefly. Attach one end of a piece of yarn to each index card label. Let children attach the other end of the yarn to the corresponding body part. Children can repeat this process to reinforce their understanding of the insect's parts. As a challenge, ask children if they can find out which part of a firefly lights up. (*the abdomen*) Share with children pictures of other insects. Let them take turns finding and identifying each part.

LANGUAGE ARTS
Make a Flashing Firefly

Make a flashing firefly for children to use as they retell *The Very Lonely Firefly* in their own words.

 **Tip**

Gather other props to use in retellings, such as a toy dog and cat, a picture of a lightbulb, a toy car (for headlights), and so on.

🌟 Line a clear plastic cup with yellow tissue paper.

🌟 Cut off the foot of a black sock. Stretch one end of the sock around the top of the cup. Use a rubber band to hold the sock in place.

🌟 Glue on two googly eyes. Push three pipe cleaners through the sock to make legs. Push another pipe cleaner through the sock above the eyes to make antennae. Cut out four paper wings and glue them to the back.

🌟 Place a flashlight in the sock. Let children retell the story, using the flashlight firefly as a prop. They can dim the lights in the room, then turn the flashlight on and off as they retell the story.

Directions for the flashlight firefly were adapted from Crafts for Kids Who Are Wild About Insects *by Kathy Ross (Milbrook Press, 1997).*

🐝 LEARN MORE

Books

Fireflies! by Julie Brinckloe (Aladdin, 1986). This Reading Rainbow book brings back the timeless childhood memory of catching fireflies.

Fireflies in the Night by Judy Hawes (HarperCollins, 1991). This introduction to fireflies explains why these beetles light up and how various cultures use firefly light.

Web Sites

The Firefly Files (**iris.biosci.ohio-state.edu/projects/FFiles/**): You'll find firefly photos, facts, and fun here (including how to attract fireflies at night).

Word-Builders Memory Game

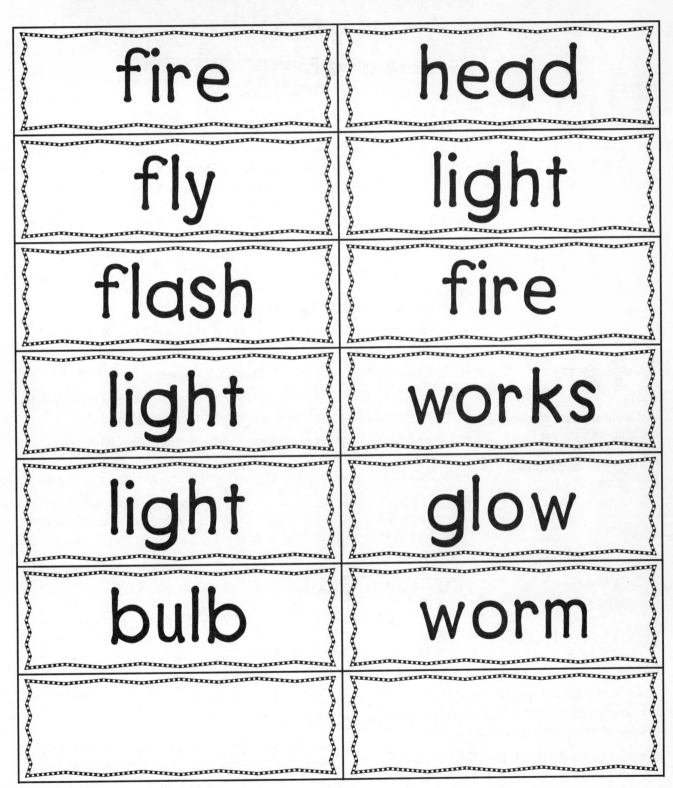

fire	head
fly	light
flash	fire
light	works
light	glow
bulb	worm

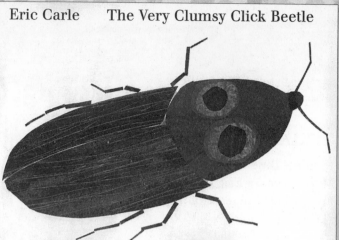

Eric Carle   The Very Clumsy Click Beetle

The Very Clumsy Click Beetle

(Philomel, 1999)

"Look at me!" a young click beetle exclaims as it flips through the air. But when it lands on its back instead of its feet, it becomes discouraged. "How very clumsy of me!" it says. A wise old click beetle and a parade of other animals try to help the beetle. But each time, it lands on its back. Then something so big comes along that when the wise old owl says, "QUICK, CLICK and FLIP!" the frightened young beetle somersaults through the air and lands on its feet. Like the other "Very" books, this one has an added surprise—as readers see the beetle flipping on the last page, they hear his clicks, too!

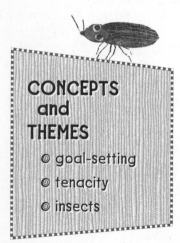

CONCEPTS and THEMES

- ◎ goal-setting
- ◎ tenacity
- ◎ insects

BEFORE READING

The "Very" Books

Which other "Very" books by Eric Carle do your students know? Let them list the main characters in the other books (*caterpillar, cricket, firefly, spider*) and share what they know about each. (See "A Quintet of Books," page 62, for a related activity.)

Stick With It!

Many of your students will be able to relate to the beetle's struggle to reach a goal, and his "stick-to-itiveness" in getting there. Invite students to share goals they've had to work hard to achieve. Then let them listen to the story, noticing how the beetle sticks to its goal.

Book Talk

In "Meet the Author" on the Children's Book Council web site (see Learn More, page 5), Eric Carle talks about the little insects in his stories. "My ittle insects are metaphors for children, who have the same problems of learning to walk, to talk, to run, or whatever. So the importance of 'stick-to-itiveness' became the theme for *The Very Clumsy Click Beetle*." After sharing the story, ask children to name words that describe the beetle—for example, *hard worker*, *persistant*, and *determined*. Discuss how these qualities helped the beetle learn to land on its feet. Guide children in discussing how those same qualities apply to their own lives.

LANGUAGE ARTS
Click Beetle Character Web

Help children learn more about the determined click beetle in the story by completing character webs. Give each child a copy of page 63. Have children write the character's name in the center space. (*Click Beetle*) In the spaces around the outside of the web, have children write words that tell about the beetle. Have children make their own webs to tell about characters in other Eric Carle stories.

LANGUAGE ARTS
"Quick, Click" Word Toss Game

In the story, the wise old click beetle tells a frightened young click beetle, "QUICK, CLICK and FLIP!" Write these words on the chalkboard and ask students to tell which two words rhyme. (*quick* and *click*) Use these words to introduce a mini-lesson on the *–ick* word family. Brainstorm other words that rhyme with *quick* and *click*—for example, *kick*, *lick*, *Nick*, *pick*, *Rick*, *sick*, *tick*, *wick*, *trick*, and *slick*. Play a game to help students quickly recognize words in this family.

⭐ Write each word on an index card. (Make duplicates of some so that there is at least one *–ick* card for each child.) Write "distractor" words (words of about the same length but without the letters *–ick*) on other index cards.

⭐ Scatter the words around a basket. Explain to students that each time they hear a clicking noise (a pen with a push-down top makes a great clicker), they need to pick up a word that rhymes with *click*, say the word, and put it in the basket. Have children take turns picking up cards (one per click).

Word Play

Write the following sentence from the book on the chalkboard: *One fine morning a click beetle decided to go for a walk.* Ask: *Which word in this sentence tells what the click beetle did?* (decided) Help children identify the root word and the ending. Revisit the story, asking children to find other words with -ed endings, including:

    climbed
    rummaged
    crawled
    flipped
    clicked

Record the words on chart paper. Guide children in recognizing the root of each word. Help children make the pull-through on page 64 to practice making and reading words with -ed endings.

✦ The first time you play, time the clicks so that they are five to ten seconds apart. Encourage children to find their words before the next click. Repeat the activity, timing clicks so that they are progressively closer together. How quickly can children identify *–ick* words?

A Quintet of Books

Gather the "Very" books together for a quintet of book studies. (*The Very Hungry Caterpillar, The Very Clumsy Click Beetle, The Very Lonely Firefly, The Very Busy Spider, The Very Quiet Cricket*) After sharing the stories, guide students in comparing illustrations, characters, themes, and so on in the books. Use graphic organizers, such as Venn diagrams and webs, to help students make comparisons. Keep these tips in mind to guide students' participation in the author study.

✦ Remind children to give each other "think time" to allow everyone a chance to contribute without interruptions.

✦ Get a discussion started by looking at the cover. Let children make connections to the other books.

✦ Let children use response journals to record additional comments about the books.

LEARN MORE

Books

Bugs! by David T. Greenberg (Little, Brown, 1997). "Beetles, bedbugs, bottle flies, tarantulas the size of pies…" Lively, rhyming text moves right along, as the author suggests one stomach-turning suggestion after another for what to do with bugs.

Bugs, Beetles, and Butterflies (Puffin Science Easy-To-Read) by Harriet Ziefert (Puffin, 1998). Beginning readers learn about beetles and other bugs in a colorful and detailed book. A glossary and Science Fun activities invite further learning.

Web Sites

National Museum of Natural History (**www.si.edu/resource/faq/nmnh/buginfo/beetle.htm**): Your students will find all sorts of amazing information at this comprehensive site. For starters, with 350,000 different species, beetles are the largest animal group. About 30,000 of those species live in the United States! What's your state insect? Find that out here, too.

Bugbios (**www.insects.org**): Click beetles, tiger beetles, whirligig beetles, blister beetles, and more come to life in big, bright photos.

Click Beetle Character Web

Click Beetle Pull-Through Patterns

Pull-Through Strip

Beetle

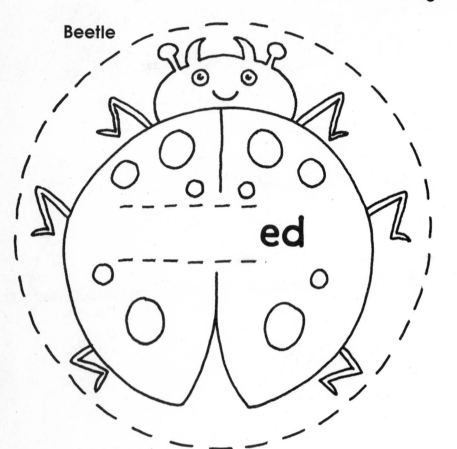

ed

climb

crawl

click

walk

jump

kick

pick

ask

play

Directions

1. Cut out the beetle on the dashed lines.

2. Cut both dashed lines on the beetle to make two slits.

3. Cut out the pull-through strip. Pull it up through one slit in the beetle. Push it down through the other slit.

4. Pull the strip through the beetle to make and read new words.

Teaching With Favorite Eric Carle Books Scholastic Professional Books